1

Table of Contents

ruminations
roo lingenfelter

to me.
if you cannot Firmly Grasp It,
put it down. move along.

a Quill who doesn't

I own a quill (soft and sharp)

She owns an ink pot (round, wet)

and I bring to life what She yearns to write.

the Words love me

They stain everything dark but

I think, still

They must be lovely to see

(I cannot read. I cannot see.)

      can you See?

                            will you tell me

                         what They mean?

can

you

read

                                   Them?

                .

                .

                .

                .

              why not?

5

.

.

.

.

.

.

.

.

.

.

.

.

.

.

.

have They meant nothing all this time?

all the dead pieces
i wish that i
could open my skull
so that i
could take my brain out
and prune it.
i would cut off all the dead pieces
all the marred and mangled pieces
inflamed and infected
by dirty-jagged edges of
shattered memories
embedded in the gray matter
and i would
throw them away
so that
when i replace my brain
and screw my skull on tighter than before
i would no longer be reminded
by their existence
how
they came to exist
within such an awful state.

does the sky make you sad?

the sky is gray today

the clouds are swollen

it rained today

again.

i love the rain. i do

if i sit inside and stare outside,

it almost looks pretty

if i'm walking outside, going somewhere

and it falls on my skin

before my eyes, in my hair,

down my cheeks, camouflaging tears.

don't you think it feels nice?

Don't you think so?

Don't you?

.

.

.

.

.

.

.

.

.

8

.

.

.

.

.

.

.

.

.

.

.

.

.

.

.

.

.

.

.

.

the sky is gray.

is it still coming down out there?

.

9

.
.
.
.
.
.
.
.
.
.
.
.
.
.
.
.
.
.
.
.
.
.

when will it stop?

what's wrong with her?

She is detached. That is what's wrong with her. She doesn't live in the world around her; she lives somewhere inside that head on her shoulders. She can't produce a single tangible thing to the world around her, because she can't seem to figure out how to translate what goes on inside into perceivable creation. It is as if she no longer speaks the language of the universe at her fingertips, no longer vibrates at the same frequency, no longer moves to the same rhythm, no longer lives by the same clock, and so she simply flounders. She is useless. She is a victim of herself, and for that, she is selfish. What a tragedy

somewhere along the lines

skipping through flower fields

staring up at a true-blue sky

somewhere along the lines, we knew

we were seeing the same images

in the same clouds.

racing through rolling valleys

laughing, breathless, all the way

somewhere along the lines, we realized

our feet were hitting the ground

in perfect sync.

throwing lit matches on land we'd covered

just to prove we conquered;

destroying the world around us

just to feel invincible

when we lived to watch it crumble.

simultaneously going down different paths

after daring the other to go first

but somewhere along the lines,

inevitably finding one another

in the same place.

somewhere along the lines, we both knew

those paths would join again.

somewhere along the lines, we realized

we would do anything to stay together,

even if it meant sabotaging our Self.

ruminations - roo

but we've done this too many times now,

haven't we?

the thrill of killing dwindles

when everything is already dead.

somewhere along the lines, I saw you yawn.

your eyes looked heavy

and it terrified me

until I noticed that I was looking

through weighted eyes of my own.

somewhere along the lines, I got tired.

I think you were tired, too.

because somewhere along the lines,

we slowed down.

we looked back

and somewhere along the lines,

we saw the same damage

we saw the same wildfires scorching

the rest of what we might've been without the other.

somewhere along the lines, we comprehended

just how easily we were desensitized

to what sparked them.

somewhere along the lines, we realized

we couldn't ever go back

but I knew you

and I could see the decision in your eyes:

despite how far we'd come,

you wouldn't be continuing on—

and suddenly,

I knew that I was alone,

next to you.

somewhere along the lines, we settled on sleep

you told me our journey wasn't over

plotting deceit while offering peace of mind

and in silence, I let you

just so I could pretend to avoid what I knew

was confirmation of its end.

eyes fell closed. tried listening

for your breaths in the ringing dark

But I was **SO** *tired. . .*

(Will you remember? Will you remember?)

and we awoke 2,000 miles apart

with lingering aches in our chests

with minds full of a past we were remembering *how*

to forget

and with the very same remnants

of the very same dream floating around in our heads.

a Writer (or the lack thereof)

the Page is empty, but here i am

    (there, i am not, but here, i am).

the Mind is quiet, but hear my footsteps:

    they do not make noise

        but if you are close, they may not be

            silent.

and if you are near, i may not be far

but if you trail behind, i won't lead you forward

    i will turn to ask why

        i will ask with my eyes, because

            my voice does not work anymore.

but you do not see my eyes

you will look to my mouth (or the lack thereof),

    and it will not open.

        it will not speak, because

        it cannot speak

            Without you.

    So you do not speak, because

    i do not speak.

        Because you do not speak:

            we do not speak

while is raised a question by the eyes you do not

see—

        i am Story, but you are not

        and you are Real, but i am not

and i could touch you,

if i could touch me (or the lack thereof),

but i cannot,

so why can you?

you do not answer;

you do not speak.

we cannot not speak

about this Space Between

(or the lack thereof)

until i spill from my seams

(or the lack thereof),

and wait to be

caught

by your words

on the Page.

but you do not catch me

i do not see you watch me

i do not hear you call me

i do not feel you want me

and though i *know you can* touch me,

you do not touch me—

the

Page is

empty, but

here I

am.

ruminations - roo

i ~~know you can~~ touch me

.

.

.

.

.

.

.

.

.

.

.

i <u>wish you would</u> touch me

.

.

.

.

.

.

.

.

ruminations - roo

.

.

.

.

why won't you touch me?

.

.

.

.

.

.

.

.

.

.

.

.

.

(or the lack thereof)

Feminine requiem for Authenticity

I extend for miles upon miles on the Surface of the

earth.

I am an open field of Potted flowers:

a flourishing variety of life, a vibrantly feminine

mirage.

I do not root them,

since I've not the facilities for Depth

only because–

the pearly-porcelain prisons in which they are Potted

would serve no other purpose,

and I am sure I simply do not wish for them to

tarnish.

–only because.

My feet are planted Delicately above the ground

My arms stretch to cover the vast space on either

side of me

My fingers probe its contents

searching, examining, counting

(It is an effort difficult to maintain;

an overabundance of variety often leads to

forgetfulness of its contents).

But I must be sure they are all present–

all of the things that I do not define which Define me

I look left, and I See

I look right, and I See

but I cannot look below

I cannot ever Know

Knowingly, I am feminine.

I am Protected.

Divinely without need, or needing to Know

Femininely dainty, daintily girly, womanly and

silly. There is triviality in femininity.

To look, but

Never to Touch.

only because–

I am sure I simply do not wish to

for fear of discovering,   *certainly,*   the

inabilities which confine me.

–only because.

I look left again

I do this because I am Certain that I Can

and I smile Prettily at my collection of identities.

they do not respond

I am pleased.

I look right again

because I am Certain that I Can

and I nod Softly at this collection of my identities.

they do not respond

I am satisfied.

I look side to side to make sure everything is as it

should be

ruminations - roo

and everything is as it should be–

that is, my collections are visible.

they are Surface

I am exactly what I say I am

because I say what I See I am

I say what I See so that

When They look, too,

They will See what I say

this way, I am true

(but never honest).

only because–

I am what I See, though never will I Know.

–only because.

the Foolish are Quite Clever

The clever creature hides in lies

  The clever creature lies and hides

but what is lying, if not

  the art of hiding?

    convincing

        Clever

  what a Clever creature.

and What is hiding, if not

    the art of self protection?

    safety

      quite clever

  that is quite the clever creature.

But

      What is cleverness,

       if not

    the art of outrunning the self?

a sort of mental cleverness

  always leaping ahead

  never experiencing what Is.

Instead, forever preparing for what is

     (Perceived)

to be.

A lie; a sort of self-told lie

   what a Foolish creature she is.

ruminations - roo

a driving emotional force

My emotions are not poetic.

(all of this is highly curated.)

They cause a great deal of conflict. Always have, and

It

never feels poetic.

I've thought I must have a great deal of power

emotionally;

it seems now, they have a great deal

of power

over me.

I wish I would have trusted myself

at a younger age.

Perhaps then, I would recognize

the raging flushed waif

berating my breasts in the bathroom.

in which my soul sings

i love seeing friendship from the outside. i love
roaming the streets of society as an observer
just for those moments of seeing a few kindred
spirits
being boldly familiar with one another–
laughing obnoxiously,
talking loudly,
walking so close together
someone almost trips,
pushing and shoving each other
in excited reactions to whatever the topic of their
conversation
may be.

Or,

similarly,
those rarer moments
of seeing two friends meet:
in the foyer at a restaurant
when the doors open
and the expressions of the entering individual
and a seated individual
shift from ones
of searching concentration
To exuberant joy
at having finally spotted the other's face;

ruminations - roo

or driving downtown,

when the car in front slows to a stop for no apparent

reason

But

before any anger

at their seemingly unnecessary lack of movement

can ensue,

a girl

comes skipping down the sidewalk

on the right

with the brightest smile

and an outstretched arm

to throw open that car's passenger

And

climb inside–

suddenly,

the muffled bass sounding

from their stereo is turned up.

they speed off in a way

that tells you

they were aware of the cars waiting behind them

But,

in your mind,

the impatience is tempered

by one lingering word:

25

·
·
·
·
·
·
·
·
·
·
·
·
·
·
·
·
·
·
·
·
·
·
·
·

"friends."

ruminations - roo

On times, I do not eat.

Where have you gone?

Grocery shopping (singular).
Down the road, not far, further down, now up
blistering heat--I am slick with it.
Pedal faster, further now, a testament
To the bones in my skin, and sprawled on the
pavement
Rest; resume.
Huffing, doubting, get there, turn here.
On an upslope, halfway is too late
And to stop,
Will not check this off.
I do not know how to stop.
A flat tire,
an empty core,
a dormant soul.
an empty core, soulless soul
A box to check.
(these worries I ease do not belong to me)
Get there.
Empty and soulless
as you are.
Uphill, all-smiles
Paper-produce exchange, and then back down

dragging rubber, screaming lungs
Home before mother.
I bought strawberries that day
how sweet they looked
rotting at the bottom of her fridge.

How could you?

I only replied.
I only returned, I received
I promised that I would be what you need
while my own garnered scorn
from me, in me, throughout *me*
What is need?
In me, an unruly creature.
Hungry, and reaching
Starving, and vicious
Voracity to be quelled in exchange for strength and
applause
A lesson to be taught.
In you, a desolation, a pity
an unfulfilled necessity,
for which somebody
is assigned fault.
To be cultivated, protected,
respected,

Cried for, lied to.
Innocence and purity
is need, in you.

Why did you?

Agency.
though They do not live,
I still speak to my ghosts
They do not speak to me.
but I think about the ways They have haunted me
(often).
Liars crave agency yet lie in their slavery
Am I a sinner, mother?
A rescind-er
Alas, I am sorry
exhausting empty quarries
a parody of
this emptiness
I am sorry there is left a nothingness
between me,
between you, in us, within us
Wherein stillness disturbs it,
Old horrors do not scare me anymore;
They do not scare you anymore
For I have done this too many times.

What has ruined, can no longer.

This is agency

I am certain

that of love, I know better (perhaps)

but not *other.*

Until then,

I'll speak with my ghosts

Unhaunted, comforted

there is sameness in the nothingness, that is

Familiar,

empty and soulless as we are.

You are tired.

of few, of me, of you, of sleep.

I am not tired

in the way you may think

if you think *You are tired*

as prescription.

I am alive, I am medicated

I exist

of course I am tired.

of course

running, standing, pedaling,

eating ; not

I am tired

That does not mean anything to me, now
or you
against me, against you.
We are tired
let us rest.

Where will you go?

does the sea of sand on the surface of the moon
turn pink
During the *strawberry supermoon?*
each grain shifting
From the inside out.
Morphing, changing, glowing
as if some foreign energy
has contaminated them, mutated them,
made them exude their alien strawberry sheen
Are they any different?
Are they any different, really?
Of course not.
they do not change;
Rather,
It is something about circumstance
And about location
about perception
about illusion.

I have understood something of that nature to be
true.

derived of Sunday Morning

I live in a world where voices speak softly
    where lovers love one another
    wholeheartedly
and those who love none rest sweetly
    unaware that love shall come,
    and sweetly awakened when she does.
I've lived in worlds defined by the texture
    of fur-lined blankets
        found in the universe of dreams
        dreamt by open eyes
    on a stained-glass Sunday Morning,
    crisscrossed by the blood
dripping from knees skidding along the blacktop.
Little legs stumble, eyes up and arms outstretched
    but god doesn't answer
    open-eyed dreamers,
        open-eyed dreaming
        while closed lips kiss prayerlessness.
    Clasped hands only give praises
    and ask with silence for guidance
so that hearts may escape in dreams
dreamt by open eyes.
I live in a world others believe exists
    which by means of belief exists
    in the minds of the believing.

ruminations - roo

only.

FOCUS

Everyone has some place else to be while they are

here.

Going, going,

they mill and shuffle and stand and sit.

Those who are sitting are assuming the places

of those who have stood to assume some place else.

They watch one another with wary eyes.

Wary eyes look every which way, going, going

hardly speaking.

Every mouth is closed

the moment my wary eyes wear into theirs.

But still, it is louder here

and the loudness is echoing, echoing–

the lack of speaking upon eye contact

creates whispers the moment eyes disconnect.

Are they whispering about what they've seen?

What have you seen?

Who have you seen?

We are dead to one another for so much of life, but

there are split seconds

in which we remember:

we are all quite alive.

In which

eyes are alight:

someone enters.

ruminations - roo

A someone here recognizing the someone there
in the midst of all this collective going;
tasting the familiarity without
hoarding the necessary time
for swallowing its stillness.
Going, going
in different directions,
discovering separate destinations,
maintaining similar objectives.
They are friends;
we are all friends that way.
No one is everyone's friend
but most of everyone has someone.
If not here, in their minds–
buried deep, or on the surface
someone is somewhere for them.
Even though this moment,
everyone has some place to be.
To always be
friends
is to achieve recurrence in someone's thoughts
before the both of you continue your going.
Always going, perhaps hoping, but never knowing.
Always going.
I suppose it is never for too *long* a time
that we remember we are all very much alive.

ruminations - roo

Why won't you stay a while?

business, business

Busybodies, hungry bodies, scholarly bodies.

Definable, desiring, satisfiable, wielding

a desire to satisfy passion–

a passion of satisfactory definition,

a passion identifiable and realized.

I wish I could be like them.

I watch them from amongst them

as if I am not. *Am I?*

There is a girl sitting at the table in front of me.

She is alone (as am I).

She is facing what I am facing,

and so we are not facing each other.

She has headphones on. I wonder

what it is she hears

in the music she chose.

I wonder what music she hears.

I wonder, I wonder

going, going

ruminations - roo

t
h
i
n
k
i
n
g
,
h
o
p
i
n
g
.

I find I am going more than everyone here
in this place, with some place else to be.

I wonder what she was doing before she
sat down, before she came here, before
she left
her home this morning.
Before she became an adult,
when she was a child.

What happened?

What ever happened to any of us?

How come we are in this place?

Always with some place else to be.

Going, going

Curious, so curious.

She has left by now: stood, walked, left.

I wonder how many times she will leave today.

Two men take her seat; they are louder than she.

I can hear them speak

What

I hear all sorts of speak, but

about

I have yet to see

this

a single mouth move. How funny

place

They are still quite loud, but

makes

they have been going, going

it

just to sit for some soft seconds,

so

loud?

I do not begrudge them.

I regard them, because,

ruminations - roo

Regardless, they will be going again

Soon.

So it goes, going, always.

Everyone else has some place to be while they are

here,

excluding my

self.

It is always going, wondering, hoping–

not moving.

Motionless motion

Because none of these connote direction

with intention.

If I stand, how do I move? Where will I walk?

What place is mine?

And if I leave where I am,

whose place will become that seat this time?

my lips are sealed

The step that you took, one

      Autumn afternoon

Toward me, so infinitesimally I could barely

        tell.

And you don't kiss, but

I wanted you to.

      I stared at your lips

          while I sealed up my own

and your lips fell apart to say something so

      sweet

that I can't remember anymore.

I haven't kissed you, but I have consumed you.

      You taste of the bitter wax coating

          congealing over the crackling, dry

                    skin

                of my lips.

                Still,

I take bite after bite, searching

for the sweet thing your lips had formed

      (once before)

and only,

I taste flesh.

            Before you are all gone,

        Once all I've left is your lips,

When I stare at them, waiting,

ruminations - roo

I think that I did not want you.

Only, I wanted

what I tasted

in the words your lips

created.

the self-inflicted Writer

There's a vacancy about the space where redundancy resides within a Writer's lines.

A broken spirit, a desolate energy produced by emotional stagnancy

What has the Writer left to give, so tired, dried, and drained by constant catharsis?

When does passion become a construction for the Page?

Creating new incisions on healed surgery sites, a skeptic of my own scars

Frustrated by the fact that they do not bleed enough anymore

Searching for fright in childlike fears I've long since outgrown

Leaving the back door ajar to beckon ghosts by which I am no longer haunted.

they never come; I cannot make them real enough anymore.

Empty, the Page remains.

But still, betrayal causes pain. Raccoons make me cry

I do not ever remember December ruining this many lives.

A Writer's line ceasing before it begins reaching reversion

Certain stars in the sky burning larger than life and
then,

Vanishing.

Perhaps there was cohesion, once, but

Details disintegrate over time, and

Now, I am just making myself sick.

Regurgitating rotten realities does not relate to the
craft of creation.

I cannot write this story anymore.

Oh no, I

I am still glancing at my shoulder.

Some times, for the road kill;

most times, I'm checking for bones.

Do you remember when I began

to hide whenever I cried

so that I could collect my tears

before you could lick them from my face?

I always considered that a repulsive habit, but

not for the obvious reasons.

The glass vial in which I kept them still sits on the

mantelpiece, and

some nights, I think of dribbling them

onto my cornea;

I think of them slithering back

into the glands behind my eyes.

I think, perhaps then, they'd fester there, and

sink into the cells and multiply,

but

most nights, I am trying to forget them,

as I find that

I cannot cry

anymore.

And on those nights, I

leave through the bulletproof glass

and float along the street,

ruminations - roo

until the headlights at my back

scatter the shadows at my feet.

Oh no, I

I don't recognize this one.

I let myself get lost, and

lie limply on the breeze,

breathing it deeply to fill this body, but

nothing ever does.

All I've done is get higher, and

these heights are making me miss

when I could cry.

My eyes are dry

from dazing while the

gusts grab at me,

gut me, but

never hurt me

because. to be

honest.

I'd rather my insides be emptied.

At least, I

I like to imagine what it would be like

if I could have wanted nothing.

At least.

things are different.

now.

ruminations - roo

Now, I

       what I've wanted most, for a long time

       is to crawl into my mother's bed, and

                  sleep

                    there

                      forever.

gravewalker

Today is a day in which I ask myself,

     "Why do you stroll the cemeteries

     and cry for lack of life?"

They house graves, grieving girl

in which the dead are put away

to rest, for they have lived.

They cannot provide relief for your refusal.

Why must you exhaust them so?

Frivolously, you check and inspect each tomb,

frantically hoping for emptiness

an empty place to lay your tired head,

and take the place of the risen dead;

To fill the casket with your corpse instead, empty all

the while–

you have been, for years.

Too many strolls down long, wrong paths

that wind through dry lands with no way back.

Purposely unprepared, a sort of self punishment

to be so reckless.

Balance seems hard to come by these days, as is

sanity.

You entertain delusion; the dead do not rise.

You extinguish yourself with glee

Hoping, in the meantime,

                        Maybe here.

ruminations - roo

Maybe this time.

Today is a day in which I demand of myself,

"Why must you waste away,

awaiting your hour in the grave?"

quick lesson

a blackest heart sloughs off the days and nights of
gold
shuffling inward through thick sleeves of snow
slovenly, is she? all bruised and beat
she shivers here, and hates it
misses when the sun would scream at her face till
she flushed red
says sweat streaming down her sides sounds nice
funny, how much we mind.
well, hotter months were months ago
petrify now, and don't feel so sorry for it
Stupid one.
the skies, pallid and sick like she
they will not watch over her.
when is it that the eyes begin to bulge?
the duller days tighten them
they start easily, shift with urgency
scan paper skins, etch brains onto these things
can't seem to see very clearly.
unaccounted spaces gape, looking back, but
flourishing and *withering* have always sounded
strangely synonymous
where has transition hidden?
progress has disintegrated

This has been sudden.

ruminations - roo

indecision about doomsday

who will you love with that

heart in your chest

bent on bleeding for nothing?

She is yearning for

no one in particular.

She is so particular but

she tells no one, and watches

anxiously, instead, as things

happen;

any old thing happening;

just something happening; not what

she wants;

but, then again,

What do you want?

Has she ever known?

Perhaps she is hoping that the yearning

will cost the rest of her blood;

perhaps she will bleed herself dry,

tell herself it is soothing because

She'll lose sensation without the circulation.

Perhaps that is it, then: all of her yearning;

all the calculated waiting;

all of that bleeding;

all of that screaming;

a purging for the silence that follows.

ruminations - roo

there is (Some times)
a book on the coffee table. It wears
a thin layer of dust.
I haven't picked it up
in ages, but
I remember the sound of its voice
the same way I recall my mother
sewing each of my names together with tight tones.
(It often meant I was in trouble.)
some times,
When it happens upon my sight, I am paralyzed.
I do not move, and
the day in front of me is a memory
of something I used to accomplish with ease.
I am wondering,
when will I need you again?
I am not hoping, just
waiting, which
often yields uselessness.
(I am told.)
I am told that I am waiting because I must not wish
to begin;
But if everything "good" is something to wait for,
let me escape my misery in the way I know how.
I have been waiting for so long already.
I've lost track of all that was supposed to happen

while I whittle away at the hours

with the will that created these brittle bones.

I think about beginning it again

every time I wear a new purple shadow—

that book

that doesn't always sit on the coffee table.

some times

When it listens while I ponder, watches me linger

at the edge of the living room

it tugs at my fingers

and begs for my grip.

I could never get a grip

but I could tuck it away in a bag packed for a day

in which its voice will not be included.

I do

(some times).

My mother would call it unnecessary weight,

a waste of space.

I made myself comfortable with wasted space at an

early age.

Hiraeth

The night air was thick with humidity, yet temperate. It was the kind of atmosphere that expands in the throat when lips part to draw in breath, the kind that makes clothes feel infinitesimally closer to skin, the kind that can be sensed settling very gently upon every strand of hair hanging from the head. It was sticky without venturing into suffocating, a relief provided only by the occasional breeze carefully disturbing that summer evening's stagnancy. Of relief in Nowhere, there was never much allowed—as it were, I inhaled deeply each time the wind rushed by in an effort to indulge that fleeting moment of rejuvenation before it slipped away from me, again.

I sat with my arms locked around my legs, rigidly compressing my thighs to my chest. I rested my chin upon my knees and stared up, unblinking, at the familiarity of vast blackness covering the sky and obscuring the moon's glow, as well as whatever else was supposed to be up there providing natural sources of illumination. I'd heard stories of stars and clusters of stars called constellations that people turned into shapes and images in their minds and nicknamed accordingly. I'd heard stories of the moon as a full, crisp white disc, shooting beams of angelic light down into the world below, but I'd never seen it defined much beyond the shape of a dim, gray pinprick whose blurry glimmer served no other purpose but to indicate its position in the sky. Such was the image that raptured my gaze for those few hours in which I awaited a better one.

Nova had spent the day away, gallivanting a city whose nighttime laid claim to all those sky jewels I would never be able to see for myself. I hated when he left; I hated the way I felt when he left, like my existence had reverted to meaninglessness, purposelessness, emptiness—there was a hole inside of me, a lack of substance, a lack of *being*. When Nova was around, though, so was meaning, and purpose, and substance. That hole wasn't *filled*. Rather, it became as if it had never existed to begin with.

But he wasn't aware of that, and neither could, should, nor would he ever be. I understood that I needed to tread with caution when approaching his fondness of me; I understood that my attachment to him reflected nothing about the nature of his attachment to me—or the lack thereof. Nova merely preferred me to others of Nowhere, whereas I needed his presence as though it were my daily dose of a prescribed elixir especially designed to

ruminations - roo

treat some mysterious, rapidly growing disease
inside of my chest. The difference pained me, but
what twisted my lips in unbearable agony was the
thought of him truly understanding the greatness of
such a difference. It was the thought of him
understanding me as more than he'd bargained for,
more than he wanted, *not* what he wanted.

Nova was a free spirit. He hadn't meant to be
my relief; he didn't deserve the burden I'd already
been carrying for a lifetime on top of his own. I'd long
since made up my mind to enjoy him only when he
could afford it, and to need him only when he wasn't
there to witness.

His absence weighing upon my shoulders, I
needed him that night. My perception of reality as I
knew it was so obscured without the consistency he
represented. Time did not move the same; the
meager bit of a sense of structure I momentarily
obtained around him dissipated when he was gone.
All I seemed to be capable of doing was waiting for
his return. The focus of my thoughts and mind
disobeyed any further instruction.

Earlier, hours before his departure, he
promised to bring back a picture of the moon for
me—a real picture of the celestial body as it was
supposed to appear, in the places where it still did.

He'd said it would be an image unperturbed by
Nowhere's alien sky, the contents of which had long
since been engulfed by the ultimate seize of mass
industrialism and the constant cloud of fog it
pumped into our wastelands from the societies
populating the rest of the earth, or what we of
Nowhere called *Elsewhere.* It was his way of telling
me he'd return, that he'd always return, and so there
I sat, waiting, my eyes never drifting from the
cheapened version of his promise.

It was also his way of giving me what he
dubbed a "birthday" present. He'd explained that
birthdays were celebrations held on the day of the
year in which an individual was born to
commemorate their existence; I'd stared back
blankly, unable to bring to my lips the words to say
that I couldn't remember my *birth*day, that I couldn't
remember anything about my origin, that I didn't
even know exactly how old I was. I was sure Nova
must have seen the panic on my face, or maybe it
just looked like confusion to him, and maybe that's
how I internally explained his flippantly responsive
laughter—he knew that he was the only individual
living in the wastelands with vague memories of his
childhood, with a sparse knowledge of where he
came from, with documents somewhere containing

57

information about his personhood and confirming he was a *human being* who inhabited the earth.

With access to Elsewhere.

That thought was the pointed end of a dagger's blade just barely touching my backside, and on occasion, whoever held onto it enforced a minimal, yet discernable, pressure, only to remind me that it was always there—poised to plunge, indefinitely frozen. Never because of jealousy or envy, but because that thought signified the difference between us. It signified my ignorance in stark contrast to his wit; it signified a place in which, should he go, I would never be able to follow. It signified that he had the potential to be something, and that I would always be nothing.

Everyone of Nowhere was nothing. We were the unfortunates and the unwanted, the un-aborted babies, the "population's excess." We were living, but no one had any record of it; we breathed air without really existing. We were stragglers of the wastelands, though *wastelands* is really a generous way to refer to our place of residence. Beside the general issue of overpopulation and the need for room to expand society, the reality was that dumps had grown wildly out of control decades prior, enough to be considered a hazard to the air breathed by those of neighboring cities. As a result, the powers that be decided something must be done to protect their citizens. Dumping places within societally occupied lands were outlawed, and this island was now nothing more than the world's collective trash heap. The humans cast onto this island were included in that collective.

In Nowhere, some of us were entirely nonfunctioning, suffering various debilitating illnesses of the mind and body—call it an effect of the solitude, call them simply crazy, call it a byproduct of the pollution manifesting over time or a buildup in the bloodstream and organs of whatever toxins the trash must be releasing into the air for it to be considered so hazardous. But some of us were like me—conscious and aware, perceptive and communicative with a desire to exist but without the ability to know why. Or perhaps we were just lucky enough to have been cast onto a slightly less hazardous portion of the island, an area that hadn't yet been completely overrun by the world's putrefied garbage. Those of us found one another shortly after the establishment of the wastelands—or the *Outer* Slums, in contrast to the *Inner* Society, as the regions are officially titled—over thirty years ago. They began the East and South Bands of Nowhere, communities built upon the largest Dumpster known to the planet, utilizing what they could out of junk to satisfy the most human need for a home.

I was of the South Band. Nova was an inhabitant of Nowhere, and spent most of his time in the South Band, but not for the same reason most all of us did. He'd had a life before this; he'd only lived in the South Band since the age of eleven. His mother was said to have died during childbirth, and he was forced out of society after his father filed for bankruptcy. He'd said his father was classified as *illegitimate* under bankruptcy, and that any child of an illegitimate adult was automatically cast to the Outer Slums in the name of population control and "maintaining societal standards."

Nova was twenty-two years old now. He'd been traveling back and forth between Nowhere and Elsewhere for nearly a full year, but I'd known him for five. He never went into detail about how it was suddenly possible for him to return to the mainlands, nor about why he chose to venture back to the wastelands. He'd only said he was "given an opportunity" in regard to the former, waiving its true meaning and noticeably stifling his excitement by passing it off as something to do with a law about "redemption" and the age of twenty-one. The latter was partially and weakly attributed to the South Band community, though I could sense his distance from this life of utter squalor after that first time he came back from a trip to the mainlands. Mostly, however, Nova attributed it to me. But I didn't have the strength to tell him I didn't think I was a good enough reason for him to keep coming back.

Because I don't want it to be true.

But it was, and I knew as much. I knew I should have been preparing myself for the day that I didn't hear the faintly repeating, metallic thud of his footfalls approaching me slowly from behind. He always attempted to be silent as a ghost while treading on the warped metal slab that took the place of a roof over where I typically slept—an old, creaky mattress and a crude assortment of fabrics acting as blankets wedged between the rust-damaged bodies of two scrapped trucks. But even in the instance that the sound was truly inaudible, I could always feel the slight vibration of the weight of his steps upon the metal reverberating underneath me, and he could never surprise me in the way that he wanted. I was always waiting for a tell-tale sign of his proximity, so that the moment one was revealed, I wouldn't miss it.

I knew I should have been working on loosening my dependence on those indicators of his presence; I knew I should have been trying to let him go, to disconnect, to detach. It was only a matter of time before the life he was building in Elsewhere became a greater source of fulfillment to him than I could ever hope to have the facilities for, stupid and stagnant as I'd always been, and forever would be.

But I didn't begrudge him for pursuing what fulfilled him. Were it not an impossibility for me, and should he be receptive, I would do the same.

And so, there upon that metal slab roof, I sat, waiting for any one of those indicators. I did not believe in god, or a higher entity, or a cosmic force controlling the universe, but right then, I might have prayed a small prayer to the hazy blackness of Nowhere's ominous sky for the sound of his voice to leap from the depths of this pitch and fill me with his light again. I'd known him for so long, become so accustomed to him, to his companionship in these dying wastelands and to the feeling of belonging I gleaned from simply existing alongside him—me and Nova, Nova and I, against all of Elsewhere.

But it was a child's fleeting dream, a finite stability whose eternity I'd let myself believe in for a bit too long. I could feel its rot steadily eating away at the heart in my chest just a little faster every time I tried to entertain the notion anymore.

Nova and I, against all of Elsewhere.

Going nowhere.

I hadn't accepted it, but I was also incapable of imagining a scenario in which I could fight it. In the meantime, I continued to wait for what I did still have of his commitment.

I shifted stiffly, tightening my arms around my legs and flexing my shoulder blades in a constrained stretch as the familiar sensation of my neck aching from gazing unwaveringly up at the sky persisted with increasing impetus. There were illumination towers planted here and there throughout the wastelands, and the light they emitted, combined with the frequency of their manifestation, was powerful enough to wash nighttime in Nowhere with a sickly sort of luminescence, so the contour of the world before me and its nearby contents were at least partially visible. The portion of earth on which this world survived was rock and dust, and it did not ever blossom beyond a few sparse tufts of grassweed—I had seen perhaps a handful of trees in my lifetime. The beige-and-gray color palette it wore during the weak, blighted glow of daytime rescinded into blackness tainted dimly by a sallow green when the sun disappeared; the landscape around my sleeping place consisted of mostly scrap metal and miscellaneous reject-heaps stretching for a small distance before one might run into other makeshift structures serving as homes and trading markets for "edible goods" within the South Band community. It was a depressing and inexorably desolate image. I kept my head tilted back into hunched shoulders despite the protests of my sore neck and pushed out a long breath, attempting to do something like meld my eyes to the ghostly wisp of moonlight above me.

Bbmm.

The muted sound of contacted metal rumbled so very quietly some distance behind. I felt my limbs turn to stone and my throat close as I temporarily disregarded the need for air in favor of unfiltered audible access to my surroundings. I always refused to turn, just on the off chance that I'd be disappointed by the same vacancy in which I'd been dwelling for what seemed like an immeasurable amount of time. My heartbeat accelerated nervously; I could hear and feel its pulse rattling my ear drums. My gaze was still directed at the moon, but I wasn't seeing it. I'd forgotten all about his promised gift by then. I found my thoughts repeatedly gravitating toward that prayer I'd prayed moments before, a cyclical phrase made up of the only words my mind could conjure:

Please. Please come back. Come back, Nova, come back. Please.

It was all I ever looked forward to.

When the metal beneath me shivered almost imperceptibly—once, twice, three times, in a slow, dragging procession, each successive occurrence embodying more validation for my frantic hopes than the last—I thought to myself that those prayers had been received. And when my eyesight was suddenly blocked by the unmistakable width of his palm, when a weight rested suddenly on the crown of my head, when a sturdy wall of warmth pressed gently against my backside, I knew that they had. I knew it was Nova. I knew he was there.

You're here.

An exuberant smile took place upon my lips from nothing of my own volition. Before I could even consciously make movement, my hand grasped at his bicep above my shoulder, constricting as though he might disappear as soon as he'd arrived. The sensation of his chest trembling faintly behind me as he puffed soundless laughter transformed me, and I was living again, inhaling deeply, gasping out laughter in response. Perhaps it was that my soul, that source and propellant of human sentience, had come back with him. I could easily be ignorant to his ultimate transience while suspended in the moments of his constancy.

"You're here," I breathed aloud, but barely.

With his hand still in place over my eyes, Nova lifted his chin and pressed his cheek to the back of my head instead. I felt his lips stretch into small grin, and the soul he'd returned to me soared higher than the haze of pollution obscuring Nowhere's sky.

"I'm here," he echoed. In a lighter tone, he added, "And you're here. Now we're both here. Here we are."

"Still here. Just like I said I would be." I swallowed, and the smile in my expression faltered for a split second. The correction I'd made to his wording went unnoticed by him, and had rolled unintentionally from my tongue, but the reality of its significance dawned upon me dismally. I made an arduous effort to suppress that reality as I whispered quietly, "Hello, Nova."

Above all else, I loved saying his name.

Nova chuckled through his nose and flexed his free arm around my chest, squeezing me affectionately.

"Hello, *Ma-a-ars.*" His tone lagged around the vowel of my name in deliberate exaggeration. "I have something for you."

My smile returned.

"You do?" I feigned.

"I do. Any guesses?"

"Any answers?"

"Nope," he quipped cheerfully.

I rolled my eyes behind his hand, tilting my head back slightly to make the motion outward.

"I guess that I'll *never* guess, because you're about to show me."

"Ding, ding." Nova retracted his arm from around me, presumably reaching for something nearby. "No peaking. Okay?"

I heard the sound of paper crinkling, and instantaneously, an overwhelming wave of the excitement that I had forgotten about hours ago coursed through me, raising the hair on my arms and tugging the corners of my lips further apart. I had no idea what *the moon* looked like. I'd never seen its true form before in my life, and Nova was moments from showing me.

There was a beat of silence, and then he spoke again:

"...*Okay...*?"

ruminations - roo

"*Yes*, yes, dammit, okay."

He hummed, clearly satisfied.

"Okay."

And he pulled his hand away from my face, resting it on my shoulder in the meantime.

I blinked rapidly at first, and then I widened my eyes, and then they stayed that way. My focal point was glued to the crumple-creased piece of paper he held before me—or rather, to the image the paper framed. In the center of a dark block of ink, a perfect silvery circle stared back at me. A glimmering halo of translucent light extended weakly from its defined borders, and textured, dull gray shadows freckled with sparkling spots of white decorated its grainy surface. It appeared to me as entirely otherworldly—mystical, impossible, magical.

"Pretty," was all that I could choke up.

Nova moved to sit beside me, carefully placing the moon's image in my eagerly outstretched hands. I grasped both sides of the paper as if it might fly away, studying each and every inconsistency upon the surface of that moon with unnecessary precision.

"I'm glad you like it," he murmured softly. He brought his arm back up around my shoulders and dragged me closer to his side. I sunk into his warmth reflexively, stunned. "This picture is high definition, though. I tore it out of an astronomy textbook. The features of the moon—like, those dark spots and light spots—are usually a lot less explicit from our vantage point on earth."

I paused and shifted to look up at him.

"Astronomy?" The word felt foreign coming from me.

"Astronomy." He nodded, amused by my uncertainty. "It's the study of the universe."

Nova's pale face and the mop of black hair framing it was shrouded in the darkness, but his cheeks and prominent nose caught enough of Nowhere's strange light to reveal his gentle expression. His eyes were a rich brown, so dark that they appeared black upon first glance during the day, let alone in the midst of night. I could hardly even see them, and I did not know how to place what it was they must have seen in me—right then, or ever. Yet, somehow, I could feel their intent.

It felt a bit like sorrow, and a bit like *compassion*. And in a matter of seconds, once more, my excitement disintegrated. My attention abandoned the image plastered on that battered piece of paper in exchange for the tenderness with which his eyes regarded me.

It could have been enough to make me cry,
and only when I blinked did I realize my own eyes
had, in fact, begun to sting.

Why?

That one word in the form of this vague
question was suddenly the only thing pressing upon
my mind. I could not pinpoint exactly *what* this
question referenced, but as our gazes remained
intertwined, I realized that I was not trying to. I was
only asking it, as demanded by the distance on his
face, in his demeanor—and the apology it silently
expressed.

I blinked slowly, while an indescribable
heaviness began to pool at the bottom of my
stomach. Nova's lips parted, and then closed. He
shifted. He touched a palm to my cheek, and rested
the pad of his thumb beneath one of my eyes. He
shifted again, and then his forehead was leaning
against mine very, very delicately.

I exhaled. I was shaking bitterly.

Why?

"I miss you, Mars," he rasped, and swallowed
roughly. "I mean, I—I've *missed* you."

An irony—the correction he made did not slip
past me.

"I missed you, too." I thought his eyes might be closed; mine were open, unseeingly directed at the darkness. "I'm here, though. Still here."

"Just like you said you'd be."

My jaw clenched, and my throat thickened. My internal acceptance of this human as temporary, and *separate* from me, was utterly blinding next to those words, and it was a physical pain to repeat them back to him.

"Just like I said I'd be."

My voice was nothing but a hoarse whisper outlined in a flick of my tongue. It must have finally collapsed under the weight of all that we'd been leaving unsaid.

How I wished I knew how to tell him to stay; how I yearned to know how to keep him.

Why?

An unknown period of time passed while we were frozen in that position, the wonder of his moon extinguished. I didn't know how close to morning it was when we finally moved, when Nova had wordlessly coaxed me closer and tucked me between his legs and pressed me to his chest and wrapped me up in his arms as though he could shield me from even death. But this was the way we'd always been: wordlessly connected. I hadn't the sensibility to fear for the coming morning. It was impossible to feel afraid of anything but a threat posed only by the future when the present had allowed me to find my most peaceful resting place against his body, curled up to his heart.

~*~

When I awoke to a stream of unnaturally pallid light, lying on my side atop a spongy mattress and swaddled in scrap fabrics, I was fully aware that I had awoken alone. My body did not possess the strength to do more than lie limp, but my eyes did not close again, and I did not go back to sleep. For another long stretch of time, I stared blurrily across the space before me at the soiled mirror hanging by a wire from the banged-up doorframe of a wrecked old truck.

I did not think any perceptible thoughts to myself; I could not think any perceptible thoughts to myself. But I didn't need to, and nor did I want to. It would only sharpen the onslaught of anguish I was suddenly trying very hard to ignore. Because somewhere inside of me, there was an acknowledgement of the fact that I would never see Nova again. Somewhere inside of me, there was an acknowledgement of the fact that I was powerless— utterly, and inescapably, *powerless*. This was not a

very new and tragic epiphany to me, however; it was
something I'd known for as long as I'd lived. But I
had never before felt it so acutely as I did the
morning after he'd left for the last time.

It took quite a while for me to notice the folded
paper lying beside my head on the mattress's
stained, dusty surface. When I did, I reached for it
mechanically—it was folded such that his image of
the moon, the symbol of the promise upon which he
had remained true, was hidden, and only a corner of
the seemingly blank underside of the page was
visible to me. In the same robotic manner I'd grasped
it with, I opened it, and in the same second that I
caught sight of the handwritten language scrawled
across that otherwise blank underside, I read it—
over, and over, and over, until the persistence of my
tears made the message too murky to decipher
anymore.

For Mars -
I'll always remember you.
- Nova

Acknowledgements

Chase Atlantic. Melanie Martinez. Etta Marcus. Beach House. MUNA. Cigarettes After Sex. Imogen Heap. Ethel Cain / Miss Anhedonia / Hayden Silas Anhedönia. Dayglow. ROLE MODEL. Miley Cyrus. MARINA. Emarosa. Ayesha Erotica. Billie Eilish. Future. Charlie xcx. KOKAYNA. Kali Uchis. Tove Lo. Mac Miller. Ariana Grande. SZA. Layzi. dylan lotus. Ricky Montgomery. TV Girl. vvherearewe. heffy. Cavetown. Bedroom. re6ce. Elita. beabadoobee. girl in red. Lana Del Rey. dolldamage. cvpidd4. cholorofilm. billyxo. Novo Amor. Lav. Clairo. Raveena. Sab Zada. Rigby. dacelynn. Lennon Stella. NIKI.

freaks x in my head – surf curse x bedroom

Rin. Who would have thought we were going to be okay? I'd say you're more to thank for that than I am. You are stronger than anyone I've ever known. You've taught me more than a degree ever could. I love you eternally, always and for infinity.

www.ingramcontent.com/pod-product-compliance
Lightning Source LLC
Chambersburg PA
CBHW061715120626
46550CB00003B/1226